FIXER

FIXER

EDGAR KUNZ

ecco

An Imprint of HarperCollins*Publishers*

HarperCollins books may be purchased for educational, business, or sales promotional use. For information, please email the Special Markets Department at SPsales@harpercollins.com.

Ecco® and HarperCollins® are trademarks of HarperCollins Publishers.

First Ecco paperback published 2023

FIRST EDITION

Designed by Angela Boutin

Library of Congress Cataloging-in-Publication Data has been applied for.

ISBN 978-0-06-328859-1

23 24 25 26 27 LBC 6 5 4 3 2

for K

CONTENTS

DAY MOON

After I left I waited for someone
a friend or her herself to walk

quickly up to me on the bus or in
the bustling coffee shop and slap

my face spit on my hands call
me a bastard a real motherfucker

by waited I mean I wanted
to be revealed by some visible sign

a welt to ride the ledge of my cheek
through the glass-littered

streets it didn't come and it didn't
come and I grew desperate I stared

too long at strangers at Safeway I bought
boxes of clementines and ate them

like a possum on the train cramming
the rinds in the gap between the seat

and the wall I drank warm beer I made
no calls I sat on a hot metal bench

by a briny lake and tried to imagine
the lives of the joggers

passing in front of me their joys
their sicknesses and regrets it was

melodramatic I was useless I thought
of my friend who wrote a novel over

a long winter in Nova Scotia
read it once and buried it in the copse

of birches behind the house he chose
the spot he said for its plainness

so he couldn't remember later
and dig it up and in this way one

medicated season slid into the next
without incident gardenia bloom

persistent sun I fell in love
with the perfect voice of a Midwest

radio DJ from a station I streamed
on my phone called in one request

after another I fell in love with a video
of Stevie Nicks singing backstage

to her makeup artist sheer
cotton dress their harmonies breezy

and immaculate I woke around noon
to the thup-thup of helicopters and another

unsober voicemail from my dad angling
for a loan went out in my underwear

and found a fine black powder settling
on the windowsills dusting the parked

cars a day moon suspended
in orange haze it turned out a man

who would go months without
getting caught was methodically setting

fire to the half-built condo complexes one
by one one in ten thousand residents

is a billionaire the same article
told me though I could be forgiven

for thinking the headlands were
burning again the intervals between

disasters collapsing I caught
my neighbor's eye she was stretching

on her stoop in a fantastic powder-
blue tracksuit what a world I said

and she didn't seem to hear and jogged
across the narrow street the moon

behind her rising or sinking
or neither it was hard to know

TESTER

I catch a bus out to the county
and check in at a beige terminal

and they ask me about the smells
and textures of various dips

and I click appealing
or not appealing, then elaborate

in the text box below. Artichoke
and French Onion. Spicy Three

Bean Queso. I got in
on referral. I live with seven

other people. I measure rent
in how many sessions I have to do

with the dips. I start testing
what I can get away with: *notes*

of bright espresso, mouthfeel
of a sun-ripe plum.

I write longer and longer.
I don't think they read a word.

It's weeks before you're entered
into the system, more weeks

to get your tiny check. Aline says
If you think it's a scam

why do you keep saying yes?
In the fluorescent room I receive

one dip after another from blue
gloved hands, always the same

plain tortilla chips to dip with,
the same hands clearing away

the tiny plastic cups. I tinker
with my descriptions. If I need

water, they bring me water
in slightly larger cups.

MODEL

In a button-up and jeans I pretend
to pump unleaded into a rented Civic.

In a peacoat and slacks I pretend
to pump premium into a rented Benz.

Inside, I stock the already stocked
shelves: SunChips and Snickers,

jumbo packs of bottled water, Powerade,
Coke. I wear an XXL polo with the excess

safety-pinned behind me, JASON stitched
in thick gold thread above my pocket.

I smile. I laugh without sound.
When this is over, I will be paid

in gas station gift cards I'll use to fill up
the car I borrowed to get here.

Meanwhile, customers come and go:
quart of milk, quarter tank, pack of smokes.

Now and then we have to ask the actual
Jason to please stay out of the shot.

ACCOUNT

Because I was the one to end it,
and so soon, I offered to reimburse her

what I owed. She had covered
most of the wedding, the move,

our rent. I was living on the grace
of a friend, sleeping

in his sunroom on Folsom.
Every morning I opened my account

to see how little I had left.
It wasn't looking good

until she wrote to say we could forget it
if I would let her claim me

on her taxes. I guessed there was
a rebate for this kind of thing.

I could hear my friend knocking
around in the kitchen, making coffee,

frying eggs. I couldn't believe
my luck. I let myself be claimed.

SHOULDER SEASON

Cutting glass from sheets
wide as twin beds to replace

the island's blown-out panes,
I drag a scoring knife

along the Sharpie line, slide
the block under, and let

each plate drop, gently,
so they break clean.

A few weeks in I begin
to get a feel for it.

I go from cottage to empty
cottage, thumb the glazing,

hide the seams. Cormorants
on the far rocks shaking out

their wings and calling.
Late sun striking the Atlantic

like a gong. Running out
of windows, I slow my pace,

make sloppy cuts I know
won't fit. I smash them out back

then call in a shipment
from Portsmouth and spend

the day imagining fresh glass
riding out on the single-

engine boat, nested in cotton
blankets in the hull.

How long can I go on
not finishing? Radio says falls

are lasting longer and longer.
The weather could hold.

WILLROBOTSTAKE
MYJOB . COM

The About page tells us
half of all human
employment is susceptible:
forklift operators, retail clerks
and manicurists. I am not
any of those things, but I am
not comforted. For each
occupation, the site assigns
an automation risk score.
Car salesman: ninety-six.
Umpire-slash-referee:
ninety-four. Each score
has been assigned a cutesy
translation—anything above
ninety: "You are doomed!"
The data scientists
who run the site deployed,
they say, a machine-learning

algorithm to calculate
the odds. The robots, then,
are making it clear exactly
which jobs they will take.
They assess each
according to the qualities
required: finger dexterity,
social perceptiveness,
originality, persuasion.
I am surprised to find
that the qualities I think of
as distinctly human
pose little challenge:
the robots are confident
in their ability to perceive,
to persuade. I click away
and click back, distracted.
I check my phone. The site
assumes a horizon
of twenty years. The AC
rumbles on as scheduled.
Something in the house dings.

REAL MONEY

Late June and there's a shortage
of air traffic controllers

in the mid-Atlantic, ads plastered
everywhere I look. *Competitive*

Pay, Union Benefits. I already found
a job, but I can't break the habit

of hunting. I dig around and learn
that though the suicide rates

are astronomical, shifts are one hour
on, one hour off, due to the extreme

concentration required. You get paid
both hours. My uncle used to work

for a company that was contracted
to paint all the nuclear power plants

in Massachusetts. Now he works
for a company that's contracted

to paint all the T stops
in the greater Boston area.

They paint overnight when the trains
are stabled. Beats the shit

out of my last job, he says, plus
they got Ping-Pong tables

in the break room at every station.
They're meant for the conductors,

he says, but hey, what they don't know.
My youngest brother quit his job

as a janitor at a middle school
to start a landscaping company.

Bought a crew cab and a trailer
and a used ride-on mower he got,

he says, for a bargain. He's staking
signs, building a client list—

mostly mowing, residential.
No 401(k), he says, but at least

I set my own schedule. I take the day
when it rains, except to pry off

and sharpen the mower blades,
file down the burrs. Dullness

tears the grass. When you do it right,
it's like you went out on your hands

and knees and snipped each tuft
with a pair of scissors. But fifty a pop

only gets me so far. Now it's about
leveling up. Corporate parks, estates,

colleges. Like where you work—
that's where the real money is.

GOOD DEAL

Fast light on my hands
as I peel the sticker
from an apple on the train.
Viruses, I read, are
colorless, though lab techs
will blast one with atoms
so we can see its edges.
We slow around a bend,
then gather new speed.
My lender calls to ask
if I feel good. I set my screen
to black-and-white to make
the living world more vivid.
He says to hang tight.
He assures me we can go
lower. In Springfield we swap
the electric engine for diesel,
then drag a small, dark cloud
across the Berkshires.
A stash of apples in my bag:

Galas. An Empire.
We blow through an empty
station in a mechanical wind.
A friend of mine rides
cross-country in the bellies
of emptied-out coal cars
or on a plate of steel
called a porch. He pays
for almost nothing. He's one
of my very favorite people.
I scroll through the latest
mortgage rates, having no idea
what a good deal looks like.
My sweetheart and I have
a rented apartment the size
of half a train car,
but we have a miniature
dishwasher, so we feel
we live in luxury.

SQUATTERS

First the brass lock punched out
and glinting on the stoop, a floral
bedsheet tacked in the window,
dim shapes moving inside. Then mail
in the mailbox. Freshly cut grass.
My other neighbor blasts Rush
Limbaugh reruns and loves
to corner me out front to explain
about mechanical pigeon spies,
China seeding clouds with acid rain.
World's going to shit, he says,
all around me. What about the feds
tapping our calls, I say, trying to be
agreeable. Bet your ass, he says.
They're dying to catch you slipping.
I'm broke, but I start leaving
at the curb whatever I can spare:
a bookshelf and two plastic lawn chairs,
a potted fig. I look out later
and they're gone; through the wall,

the scuff of a chair leg, laughter.
My brother comes to visit
and sleeps on the kitchen floor.
What's up with your neighbors, he says.
We put out a cut-glass punch bowl,
a watercolor map of the state
with the proportions all wrong.
In August, two cops in dress shirts
and bulletproof vests knock
on my door and ask if I've seen
any movements. Leave me their card.
My other neighbor juts his chin:
You seen them next door?
Heard they robbed some old lady.
Who said that, I say. He shrugs.
The heat swells and breaks.
An election happens. I sell my car
and sit on my stoop, chain-reading
paperbacks, trying to lose
as much time as possible.
Mom calls. Are you alone, she says.
It's about your dad. A hatchback
clatters by, dragging its muffler.
In the window next door, my fig
presses its leaves to the glass.

FIXER

We're breaking into your apartment
through your bedroom window.

The maintenance guy's ladder
is propped against the sill.

I climb the ladder rung by rung,
it shivers, I try not to look down.

A face appears in the glass.
What are you doing, the face says.

I'm looking for my dad's, I say.
I thought this was his window.

Aren't you Ken's boy, he says.
No, I say. Chris's. Oh, Chris, he says,

he's dead. I know, I say. I thought
you could be Ken's, he says.

Sorry, I say. Believe me,
the face says, not my first rodeo.

I climb down. We haul the ladder
to the next window and try again.

Better than the minivan you slept
a winter in, American Legion

parking lot, siphoning gas for heat,
but not much better. Cinder-block

apartment building on Homestead,
a couple miles from mom's. Got in

through the window. Waded through
the cans and bedding. Left it open

for the smell. Tried not to look
at the stain. Tried to be respectful

like in a museum. Stood for so long
in front of your dresser my brother

touched my elbow. Everything
we touch, you touched. Your socks.

Your coat. The cash in your pockets.
The cellophane from a fresh pack.

Zippo with a carving of a whale,
proud ship in the distance.

We should have hired someone,
I say. Me and Noah are dragging

your mattress out. Nah, he says,
we got it. We force it

through the doorway
and down the carpeted stairs.

We should have spared ourselves
the bucket of vomit,

the empty plastic vodka jugs,
the black rubber gloves the cops

left balled up on the dresser. Up
and in, he says, and we heave

the mattress over the green lip
of the dumpster. Might have been

worth the money, I say. Considering
the therapy bills later.

I'll tell you what's wrong
with us, he says, free of charge.

It surprises me how little
I recognize what's here. How long

has it been for you, Noah says.
Almost ten years, I guess.

Four for me, he says, stacking papers
in a ShopRite bag. You think mom

wants any of this, I say. Would you,
he says. I'll take whatever this is.

I hold up what looks like a mortar
made of bronze. A car starts

on the second try. The window
we crawled in through hangs crooked

in its frame. I want the sword, he says.
He points to the corner of the kitchen

where a rapier leans in its scabbard,
ornate and slim. Did you know dad

had a sword, I say. You don't remember,
he says. No. I don't remember.

I think I was in California when you died.
There's a window, the cop said,

but we can't be sure. Maybe it happened
while K and I were having sneaky sex

then linking up with friends we missed, friends
from when we used to live there.

Or while getting hammered touring
our old spots—Baggy's, Heart

and Dagger, Eli's Mile High—and we tried
to call it, but when we got back

the neighbors were still dancing in their
Halloween best, so we started swigging

from a plastic handle and sharing cigs
and shout-singing *Baby's black balloon*

makes her fly. Maybe then. Or when
a bearded man in sequins piggybacked

our friend and we reached on tiptoe
to pull ripe pomelos from the dark—

Typically we don't allow customers
back here, she says, but I'll make

an exception, since we haven't processed
the morning yet. Totes and boxes marked

DONATION are bound with rope
and stacked neatly on giant rolling carts.

There he is, Noah says, pointing to the bin
we dropped off before lunch.

We slip it out like a huge Jenga block,
unsnap the lid. We're looking

for a velvet case we heard you kept three
silver crosses in, you were always talking

about them, one for each of your boys.
Button-ups, flatware. Stretched-out

tube socks. You sure they were ever
in there, she says. Let me leave you

my number, I say, in case.
Oh, honey, she says. The chances of that.

René and I were doing some limb work,
Noah says, on the tree out front, that twisty

pine at the corner of the house, taking
a couple widows off it, and dad drives up

drunker than I've ever seen him,
or close, in a red Ford Focus, gives me

the biggest hug he can considering
he dropped twenty pounds since I last saw him,

and I'm the ground guy, holding the rope,
puts his arm around my shoulder and just

kind of stands there, neither of us
saying a word, not knowing after two,

three minutes he'll get back in the car
and drive off, last time I'll ever see him,

'cause when you're the ground guy you got
to focus on the guy in the tree, you mess up

and that limb swings out and hits the line
bang the whole block goes dark.

You got the best years of him,
Noah says, considering you're the oldest.

Luke says, He got a lot worse
after you left. Hid in the basement, pissed

in the laundry sink. Pretended to be
writing a book. He was a weak man,

he says, simple as that. When his truck
got stolen, Noah says, is my theory.

That was the tipping point. But he
got it back, I remind them, plus everyone

chipped in, all those Home Depot
gift cards. That made it worse, he says.

It was like he got smaller overnight,
like someone threw water on him.

You heard about the rest: mom
throwing him out, cops and everything.

He was Handy, he says. You were gone
by the time he turned into Chris.

Chris, she says, oh you mean Handy,
great guy, life of the party, the party

was always at his place, him
and your mom's, plus he could fix

anything, he was amazing, leaky faucet,
done, sticky door, done, lawn mower

won't start, done, and give him three
of whatever, you name it, didn't matter

if he was blasted or what, give him
a stapler, a pipe wrench, and a coffeepot

and he'd juggle them as long as you like,
and every time you'd think no way, it's

over, he's finished, he'd float
it all right in front of you, smooth

as a seal, then set them down easy one
by one, it was magic, everyone clapping

and carrying on, can't believe you
never saw it, that's how he always was.

The heart weighs 360 grams.
Stenosis in the coronary, eighty

percent occlusion. The valves
are unremarkable. The ventricles

are unremarkable. The brain weighs
1,310 grams and is normal size

and shape. The brain stem has
the usual patterns on cut surface.

Positive for duloxetine anti-
depressant in the blood. Positive

for nicotine. For ethanol.
The genitals are those of a normal

man. The scalp has no contusion.
The skull has no fracture. The mustache

is a quarter inch, the beard
is a half. The nose and facial bones

are intact. The tongue is
unremarkable. The airway is clear.

I held him together
as long as I could, she says.

He stopped working,
stopped coming upstairs.

He was like tissue paper
coming apart in water.

Like smoke in my hands.
It had nothing to do

with you, baby. You left
when you had to.

I met a woman once
who worked on pianos.

Said it was a hard job.
The tools, the leverage.

The required ear. I love it,
she said, but it's brutal.

The second I step away
it's already falling out of tune.

TUNING

I pull the last radishes,
then bed the boxes down

with hay. This is the season
of distances: weak light

in the lilacs, muffled bass
in the idling Accord.

My father a plaque that rises
barely above the grass.

That last time strangely
available: vinyl booth, castanets

from a jukebox we couldn't see
and the pale underside

of his wrist flashing . . .
Cleaning out his place,

I found a watch
in his underwear drawer,

chipped bezel, leather band
worn thin. It belonged

to his father. Once, as a kid,
I watched him press the cool

back of it to his ear, then
his cheek, I didn't understand.

I bend and gather up
the bolted kale. My old Trek

clutters the doorway, gray
flecked with gold. Another loop

I'm caught in: suffering
and calibration. The punishing

miles, then the hours adjusting
the neatly clicking gears.

THERAPY

Early snow. Garbage
trucks in the alley pushing
slush around, chewing.

Gnawed by a hundred
minor obligations, I draw
a bath, then sit on the toilet

fully clothed. I want
a therapist, I said to Meg,
smarter than me. You

charm them, she said. You
need a man, someone the age
your dad would be now.

How old would you be now?
I do the math and come up
with a number so low

I check again. Nothing
changes. I go out and drag
the bins back to the house,

then lower myself
into the lukewarm tub. I let half
the water out and turn

the tap, mixing the original
water with water that would
scald me if I touched it.

GOLDEN GATE

I could hear every bit of laughter passed
between the dishwashers of the café

I shared a wall with, and one morning,
touching that wall, felt it give wetly

under my hand. I called my landlord,
knowing the apartment above me

was vacant—a space, I gambled, larger
than the one I had, where every piece

of furniture touched. He surprised me
by saying yes, I could stay there

during repairs. I made my calculations.
You were giving up your perfectly

good spot in Denver. I had a month
to convince him to come down on the rent.

I moved my bed up but left the rest,
which workers covered with a tarp.

When the work was done, I went on
squatting in those bright upstairs rooms—

the windows are unreal, I told you—
for weeks, pestering the landlord

every few days, going to his house,
walking with him in his garden, trying

to explain. He relented at last, grumpily,
and I moved the rest of my stuff

before he could change his mind. You came
with everything you owned, and suddenly

we lived together. That first morning
you noticed a red access ladder

I had missed outside the kitchen window.
We climbed, one going first,

the other handing our coffees up
and clambering after, and that high

we could see the bell tower at Berkeley,
eucalyptuses in the hills and traffic

careening down Alcatraz, hint of salt
on the wind, and though we would leave

this place, too, and soon, when the rent,
despite our pleading, ratcheted

beyond us, if you craned your neck a little,
perched delicately in the distance—

No fucking way, you said—was the Golden Gate,
stitching the city to the headlands looming

across the bay, and we were moved
to silence by it, gripped by a pure, clear idea

beyond experience, and stood a long time,
touching shoulders, touching knees.

GRAND LAKE

In the next place they slept
with the windows open,

square-paneled panes
that faced a slope of ivy

and pine straw and swung
cleanly on their hinges,

screenless. But it felt as if
they lived underground,

a burrow across which
the headlights descending

the steep driveway just
on the other side of the wall

swept in the crisp dark,
maneuvering the gap

between buildings.
They were getting away

with something, they felt,
though he was newly

divorced and they were paying
heavily for the privilege

of this tiny ground-floor
studio by the lake.

They got to know
their neighbors some,

were invited over once
for pinot and gossip

by a woman who'd held on
to her apartment, she said,

since '98, outlasting a series
of aggrieved landlords

who refused repairs, and so
heated her few rooms

by turning her oven on high
and leaving the door open.

Mostly, though, they kept
to themselves. They were tired,

and wary of entanglement.
They worked and touched

quietly and made reasonable
requests. Each morning

they took their coffee out
to the garden, which did not

belong to them. At night,
the wheels, which could crush

so easily, passed inches
from their sleeping heads.

DOORS

We get them from warehouses
at the edge of the city, paging through

upright stacks, slumping one
heavily against the others and breaking

out the tape measure to see, or if
it can be made right with a table saw

and a chisel. It's mostly my thing—
K goes along, even spots the one

for the bedroom, cut-glass knob
catching light as it swings.

She knows the doors we have are fine.
They open freely, they latch closed.

She also knows I'm a maniac who can't
be stopped. She drags out a paneled turn-

of-the-century oak with mismatched
knobs, a half-length insert of beveled

glass. We lean it against the others,
her outline distorted by the waves.

NEW YEAR

Hungover and regretting
my every idiot decision, I slip out
for a smoke, startling

my neighbors, who appear
to be tearing off their back porch
with a crowbar and a hacksaw.

A new year and not much
to show for it except a sore
lower back, an addiction

to trash TV and Russian novels
on tape—I stopped reading
the news, stopped calling home.

I recused myself. Even this
soft pack isn't mine, forgotten
by a friend in the late stages

of a party cranked to eleven
by the sublimation of despair.
I should be grateful,

I guess, for the bright
morning, the smoke that makes
my breathing visible. And they

seem happy. My neighbors.
Good for them. High
on their ladders, backlit by fog.

A growing pile of scrap
in the slush below. They cut
wildly, clanging against the rungs,

it's thrilling to watch.
Sawdust gathers in the creases
of their jackets. Where they pry

the rotten timber away,
the brick is a brighter
shade of red beneath.

NIGHT HERON

What now? You'd flown in
from a Midwest city named
for its rowdy summertime
abundance lying saying you
were coming to visit friends
in San Francisco and I had taken
the train from chilly Oakland
to meet you and we rode north
carefully not touching I took you
to the tiny one-room apartment
I had escaped to after the
divorce and fried us nervously
some potatoes in a cast-iron pan
a little rosemary which we
did not eat because you kissed
me hard and we went in a rush
to the mattress I bought off a guy
in a semi-famous band and had only
the day before gotten off
the floor and onto the pinewood
bed frame I'd found and hoisted

on my back and carried
down out of North Berkeley arms
wide weaving through the side
streets toeing the centerline to avoid
snagging the buckeyes leaning out
it was about suffering
in public it was dramatic
sure but the dramas of my life
those days were pitched
as high as I could stand higher
sometimes I said breathless *I want
to taste you* and you said *please
yes* and later out at the edge
of the lake huddled against
the damp wind hot grease
soaking through a paper bag
licking salt from each
other's fingers obscenely a night
heron peered up at us from
the reeds small hunched dipping
its shining beak in the shallows not
particularly beautiful but a heron
nevertheless the same one
we were sure we saw perched
on the awning outside the theater
whose marquee shouted slogans
like WE LIVE IN A FAKE
DEMOCRACY and PREVENT UN-

WANTED PRESIDENCIES
WITH HAND COUNTED PAPER
BALLOTS and later the cabin
we rented with friends
in Calaveras snowmelt vaulting
the redwoods to magnificent
heights drinking rye and each
of us practicing our best
wolf howl at the waning
moon which was ridiculous yes
but once we started it became impossible
to stop waking up next morning
hoarse and happy and you moved west
and we lived together in a studio
overlooking the café dumpster
and then back east on a dream
of a house and a garden and then
my father died and at almost
the same age yours did and both
from drink and an unnameable
sadness I went back to Connecticut
alone three and a half days
my mother said before anyone
had found him in his apartment
on the far side of town and going
with my brother which we
should not have done and dragging
the mattress out and clearing

65

the maggots off the ceiling
with a shop vac and so on and later
you came and we walked through
the basement of my mother's house
I wanted to show you where for
a while he lived and how and you
slung your arm around my waist
and we moved slowly together bare
fluorescent bulb shining
on the Budweiser ashtray
the carpentry tools I would
inherit the ratty couch he crashed
on for years you held up
an old calypso record he loved
and sang out softly *Jump in the line*
rock your body in time and I
sang back softly *Okay I believe you*
and after a while mom at the top
of the stairs shouting *What*
are you kids doing down there
and climbing the steps you pinch
my elbow and ask if I'm
okay and I hear myself
say yes which is not a lie though
I'm not listening I'm letting
myself feel how astonishing how
astonishing what our love can make
of a place like that

MISSING IT

It's a new life: the tidy
brick bowfront joined

to its neighbors, the long
yard clotted with ivy

and vasevine we tore out
and burned in a heap,

edge of her shovel turning up
a Twix wrapper, shards

of brick, a marble made of hot
pink plastic. We miss

our old city, we say:
the poppies bushing up

at the light posts, throwing
the windows wide to let in

the cold, the high
electric whistling

of the rails—and the light,
we say, god, the light

most of all. We miss it,
we say, hammering

garden boxes together
from a friend's trashed fence.

The light—as we plant squashes
and peas, and give them

a trellis to climb.

ACKNOWLEDGMENTS

Gratitude to the editors of the following publications in whose pages these poems first appeared:

American Poetry Review
    "Night Heron"
    "Tester"
    "Shoulder Season"
    from "Fixer" [We're breaking into your apartment]
    from "Fixer" [It surprises me how little]
    from "Fixer" [I think I was in California when you died]
    from "Fixer" [Typically we don't allow customers]
    from "Fixer" [You got the best years of him]
    from "Fixer" [Chris, she says, oh you mean Handy]
    from "Fixer" [The heart weighs 360 grams]

The Atlantic
    from "Fixer" [Better than the minivan you slept] as "Museum"

Los Angeles Review of Books
    "Day Moon"

The New Yorker
    from "Fixer" [I held him together] as "Piano"
    "Therapy"

Oxford American
    "Real Money"

Pioneer Works Broadcast
    "Golden Gate"
    "Grand Lake"

Poetry
   from "Fixer" [René and I were doing some limb work]
   from "Fixer" [We should have hired someone]

Smartish Pace
   "Missing It"

What Things Cost: An Anthology for the People
   "Model"

The Yale Review
   "Tuning"

Thank you to the National Endowment for the Arts and the Maryland State Arts Council for the support that made many of these poems possible.

To the first readers of these poems for their advice and encouragement, especially Sam Ross, Megan Fernandes, Brian Tierney, Will Schutt, Hafizah Geter, Grady Chambers, Mikko Harvey, Rosalie Moffett, Callie Siskel, Noah Warren, Phillip B. Williams, and my brothers, Luke and Noah Kunz.

To Tim Weed and Julia Jensen, for the gift of those January days in which this book began to reveal itself.

To my former teachers, especially Mark Jarman and Elizabeth Spires, for their continued guidance.

To my editor, Jenny Xu, and my agent, Rob McQuilkin, whose faith in my work has been life-changing.

To Anders Carlson-Wee and Sam Cheney, whose patience and vision shaped this book profoundly.

And to my love, Katie Moulton, who astonishes.